Life is as Magical as You Make It

LEARN TO LISTEN TO YOUR HEART AND FIND YOUR JOY

Michelle Nelson-Schmidt

Joy creates magic! ♡ Michelle Nelson-Schmidt

Michelle Nelson-Schmidt
MNS Press
Pensacola, Florida
Books@MNScreative.com

Life is as Magical as You Make It: Learn to Listen to Your Heart and Find Your Joy / Michelle Nelson-Schmidt - 1st ed.
Paperback ISBN 978-1-952013-71-3

Contents

Dear Future Michelle
and Future You - who is about to
read this book,

I wrote this book for you and
dedicate it to you.

No matter what has happened or will happen, know I am proud of you. You may have made many mistakes along the way, but no one can ever say that you didn't always try your hardest to be a better person than you were the day before. Please give yourself grace and be patient–you are doing the best you can. Reread the words on these pages when you've lost your way, can't feel your joy, or don't see the magic you create in the world.
I love you dearly, beautiful soul.
Don't forget how much you matter.

"I have met my self and I am going to care for her fiercely."

—Glennon Doyle

Author's Note

My name is Michelle Nelson-Schmidt. You've probably never heard of me—totally okay. There are a gazillion people in this world. Why would you know me? So let me tell you a little bit about myself and why you should read my book.

I'm an author and illustrator of thirty-two children's books. However, I don't write books just for children; my books are for everyone. I often tell people I really write self-help books that happen to be five hundred words or less. I finally decided to write a book just for adults and any children who might want to read it too. My messages are universal. They're for all of us, and they're most definitely for you, my dear reader.

While I am not someone with a lot of letters after my name (for those of you who are, please know I am very impressed by your dedication to learning), I am still an expert. I am an expert on what I have learned from living in this beautiful yet often cruel and heartbreaking world. I've done so much, and I have had the privilege of meeting so many incredible people who have helped shape me into the expert that I am.

Every single one of us has a story to tell. Every single one of us is the expert on our own lives. I believe that if we could hear the stories of people we dislike, don't understand, or even hate, we could no longer hate. I believe it is almost impossible to hate anyone once you hear their whole story. Because with every story comes understanding, compassion, and empathy.

We all have a story to tell. Here is mine. I hope with all my heart that it helps you remember how incredible and magical your story is too.

Introduction: What This Book IS NOT

Spoiler alert! This book is not going to tell you how to become a millionaire from your hobby or your side hustle. It's not going to tell you how to get more Instagram or TikTok followers. It's not going to tell you how to get more money, more prestige, or more power.

However, this book will help make you a happier, more joyful human. I wrote this book because our world is too full of negative messages: we are not enough, we need to do more, and we need to have more to be happier.

I strongly disagree. It's so much simpler than that.

I'm giving you the answers to a happier life right here in these pages. As you read this book, you will find the answers you are seeking.

I hope you will feel the belief in yourself and your worth growing as you read my words. I hope that feeling of 'enough-ness' will fill your soul with each turn of the page.

Actually, I can guarantee it.

How, you ask? Because you are already enough. We all are. Maybe you just forgot for a while because our world makes a whole lot of money on selling you messages that you aren't enough. But you are more than enough. I am here to help you remember that for the rest of your life. My clear, simple messages in a quick, easy-to-read book will leave you smiling and feeling pretty darn good about yourself. I promise.

If you'd like to join me on this journey, then get a cup of coffee, tea, soda, or whatever beverage makes you feel cozy and happy. I want you to imagine I am sitting right across from you in a coffee shop or on your front porch. Or maybe you came to visit me at Whatif Acres. We are cozied up on my living-room sofa, and I'm about to tell you a story about me. Don't be surprised when you see yourself in my story. You will be reminded about how very awesome and magical you are—and always have been.

I've learned a few things in the fifty years I've been alive, especially the last twenty. And most definitely, this past year. It's been a *doozy*, my friends.

Comfy? Good.

Let's go.

"I am not what happened to me,
I am what I choose to become."

-Carl Jung

1
A Spark of Hope

I'VE ALWAYS LOVED PICTURE books. In particular, the kind that you randomly pick up to read quickly in a bookstore or gift shop. As you finish it, tears well up in your eyes because the message touched you so deeply—as if the author had written it just for you.

Around twenty years ago, I found a tiny red picture book like that. It had a sheep on the cover and was simply titled, *Selma*. I was out with my friend, Tammy, and we were window-shopping during a girls' day out. At the time, I was a young mom in an unhappy marriage and had no extra money for books. We were very financially insecure. We were barely scraping by and using food stamps to survive. I worried day and night about money and how we didn't have nearly enough of it.

My boyfriend and I got pregnant at the end of art college. We were young and neither one of us had gotten a job yet. We never really managed to get ahead after starting so far behind.

I remember the day before my son, Noah, was born. I pawned every piece of jewelry I'd ever been given just to make sure there was food in the kitchen when our families arrived for his birth.

The night we brought our son home, I went into my bedroom closet, put a pillow to my mouth so I wouldn't wake my newborn and boyfriend who were both sleeping a few feet away, and scream-sobbed until I couldn't breathe. I was absolutely terrified because I had no idea how we were going to make it. I'd had a baby with a man who didn't seem to want to work for his family and I had no job. Shame filled my body on a cellular level. What kind of mother was I going to be if I could not even afford to have a refrigerator full of food?

I felt lost in the world and I had no idea what my future would hold. I tried to be optimistic, but I felt like I was at the bottom of a deep hole that I had dug with every poor decision I had made in the past few years. The light at the top of this hole seemed extremely far away.

But when I picked up that little red picture book with the sheep on the cover, I felt a spark of light flicker deep inside me. The price of the book was $7.99. Normally my guilt over spending any money on myself would have made me set the book down, but I had to have it.

Selma was written by Jutta Bauer. In the book, a dog can't seem to handle life anymore. He climbs a mountain top to ask a wise old ram a simple question: 'What is happiness?' To answer, the ram tells the dog a story about Selma, a mama sheep.

Every morning at sunrise, Selma would eat a little grass, play with her children until lunchtime, exercise in the afternoon, eat some more grass, have a little chat with a neighbor in the evenings, and then finally fall fast asleep at night.

Asked what she would do if she had more time, Selma said she supposed she would eat a little grass, play with her children until lunchtime, exercise in the afternoon, eat some more grass, have a little chat with a neighbor in the evenings, and then finally fall fast asleep at night.

Asked what she would do if she won a million dollars, Selma considered it. She replied that she'd love to eat a little grass, play with her children until lunchtime, exercise in the afternoon, eat some more grass, have a little chat with a neighbor in the evenings, and then finally fall fast asleep at night.

That was the end of the book.

I cried when I read it. *Selma* spoke to my soul. That book became my definition of success. That's the life I wanted.

I wanted to create a life where even on my hard days, I was enough. To know I had enough and that I loved simply getting to be me in this life. I didn't want to be "saved" or win the lottery. I wanted to be me and to truly find joy in my life. While I wanted financial security, I also knew that I didn't want to equate my bank account with my success as a human.

I simply had to have it. I bought the book and carried it with me in my purse from then on as a reminder of what I was striving for.

I had quite a ways to go to get there, but a spark of hope had been lit. A ray of light seemed to shine down into that hole and touch me the day I read *Selma*.

"...and I think to myself,
what a wonderful world."
-Louis Armstrong

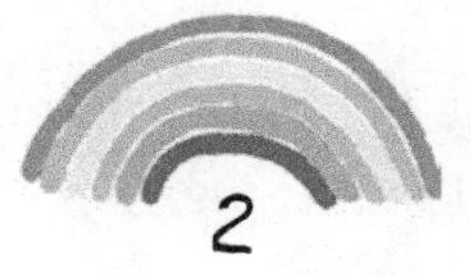

2

A Life Worthy of Selma

I FINALLY GOT TO THAT place of joy and peace—to a life that I like to think Selma herself would have liked to live. It's been quite an adventure that took a move, another child, and a painful divorce, but I got there.

Despite promising myself that I never, *ever* would, I married again to a wonderful man named Kevin. We shared custody of my children with their father who lived nearby. We all raised the children together and I was in love and happy. Years later, once the children were done with college, my husband and I moved to Florida to be near his parents, Judy and Tom.

A lot has happened in the short amount of time since we moved to Pensacola. My parents moved down a year after us to live across the

street. Then my husband's parents both passed away in the fall that same year.

My brother-in-law, Michael, who had been the main care-taker for Judy and Tom for the eight years before they passed, discovered he had Parkinson's Disease. I'd become good friends with my husband's brother through the years, and I promised Michael that he would never have to worry about where he would live after Judy and Tom were gone. I helped him find a small apartment to move into, but Kevin and I knew eventually he'd need to move in with us once his condition worsened. My father's worsening mobility issues and the stairs in their home became more and more of a hazard. It became apparent to me and my husband that we needed to find a living situation that would accommodate all of us sooner than later.

With all the moving we had just done, and because my husband does not enjoy change, I promised him I would not look for properties until it was absolutely necessary. I wanted to keep that promise. I really did.

Here's a crazy part of my story. Years earlier, I had driven down a dead end street three miles from our house. I was on my way home, and had no idea why, but I felt absolutely compelled to turn down this particular street. I sat in my truck at the end of the cul-de-sac and felt an overwhelming message telling me I needed to live on that street. This was an *insane* message. My husband and I had just really settled into our dream home, a beautiful town home on the water. *Why on Earth would we move?*

But the feeling was compelling. As I drove down the road to leave, I looked at every house. There were only twenty houses on the street. As I got to one particular house, I said aloud, "Fine. But if we need to move, then *that*'s the house I want." I drove home and forgot about it.

That was three years ago.

Now, I had *just* promised I wouldn't look for new properties. Literally the very next moment after I made that promise, I checked my email. My jaw dropped. There, in an email from Zillow, was the house. *The* house. The one I said was the only house I was willing to live in if we had to move.

You know I broke my promise to my poor husband, right? But who am I to argue with fate?

My husband didn't care for my fate argument. And I maybe dragged him to the open house with me that weekend. I like to think it wasn't *me* who dragged him, *it was fate*. (He says it was definitely me.)

We made an offer a week later.

In June of 2021, we moved into the ranch-style house I had picked out that random day three years prior. It was on a five-acre property and perfect for our multi-generational family. Yes, we all moved once again. It was a bit of a financial stretch for me and my husband. While it was *my* dream home, it was an older home that needed work, and was definitely *not* my husband's definition of a dream home. It caused some stress and anxiety, but family means everything to us and we knew it was worth it.

I pronounced our new home Whatif Acres. It's the most magical place I've ever lived. My parents moved into an in-law suite at one end of the house and my husband and I moved into the other part of the house. We remodeled a barn on the property into a private living space for Michael, who is still in very good health, thank goodness.

Once we were all settled on Whatif Acres, I took out a business loan to build a studio at the back of the property. I'd never had a true studio space to call my own before and with all the land we had, it was the perfect opportunity to build one. I now work at a desk each day that has a view of a pond filled with fish and turtles that I feed each morning. My dog, Piggy, always by my side, suns himself outside the studio door or can be found snoring in a chair in the corner. It's Heaven on Earth.

Just when I couldn't imagine life getting any better, it did. My daughter, Sophia, and her husband, Max, moved into our old house that we'd kept as a vacation rental. When they become pregnant with their first baby, we offered to let them rent it. Shortly after moving in, my precious granddaughter, Sage Louise, made her arrival. I cannot believe I am lucky enough to have the three of them only 3 miles away. My son, Noah, is only six hours north in Atlanta. I talk to him almost daily, and we visit as much as possible.

My husband, Kevin, is my opposite in almost every way. Our marriage has been a challenge at times because we see life so differently, but we would not have it any other way. We created a beautiful life together because of who we both are. Marriage is not for the faint of heart, but when you find the right person, it's worth the work. Especially when you find a person who not only allows you to grow and change as you get older, but is also someone who helps you become a better human being. I like to think we do that for each other, even if most days we roll our eyes at each other in exasperation.

The life and career I've created for myself in the years after reading *Selma* have been truly magical. I worked incredibly hard. Although most days it didn't even feel like work–I've just been doing what I love.

But during 2022, my life began unraveling. Being the eternal optimist, I kept working hard to keep my life intact, to stay afloat, and to keep my positive outlook. I knew it would all be okay as long as I kept believing in my magic and looking for joy. That had *always* worked before.

Until the day it stopped working, I lost my joy completely, and couldn't feel my magic at all.

A Life Worthy of Selma

"It's failure that gives you the proper perspective on success."

-Ellen DeGeneres

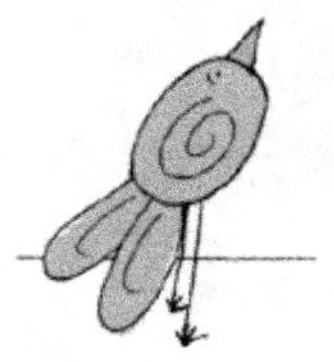

3

And Then It Was Gone

TO EXPLAIN WHAT TRANSPIRED in the past year of my life, I have to bring you back a bit, back to COVID-19. This is the longest chapter of the book, but I really want you to understand what happened to me. Buckle up, Buttercup! Here's where that doozy of a year comes in.

I want to make it clear that I'm in the middle of this journey, not yet on the other side. I didn't want to wait to write this book until I felt whole again. I wanted to write it while I'm still shattered. I wanted to write it as I'm putting my pieces back together. I could have skipped this entire chapter and only told you about my sunshiny, happy bits. It would have been a light, inspiring read. But I wanted to tell you the truth. My truth, my whole story.

During COVID, I wanted to use my free time wisely. I decided to self-publish an early reader chapter book series. I was beginning to feel a lack of control and loyalty from my publisher. They had not said yes to any new book pitches of mine in several years. I began to feel that by limiting my publishing through them, maybe I had too many financial eggs in one publishing basket.

I had really wanted to pitch the inclusive and diverse early reader series to my publisher, but frankly, I didn't want to face yet another rejection from them. I thought self-publishing the 18-set series would not only add another income stream, it would also keep me busy. I could no longer schedule my beloved author visits at schools during the pandemic. Plus, I could write about the subjects I knew children wanted to read about and the characters they wanted to see in books–without any 'editorial politics' getting in the way. I wasn't too worried about losing my school visit income because my book sales were doing very well at the time.

However, as I focused on self-publishing, I became more focused on making money. I made the most money I had ever made in 2020. People were stuck at home, and parents were buying books—lots of them. My royalties were at an all-time high, and my own self-published books were in high demand as I released them a month at a time for 18 months.

Ironically, my life felt flip-flopped. During COVID, while the world was being devastated, and others were experiencing terrible hardships, I was in a bubble of success. I watched the news every day, my heart breaking at the stories of death, job loss, and the financial insecurity of others. I ran fundraisers, sent money to friends in need, and donated to one Go-Fund-Me after another. I was thrilled with my self-publishing successes, the growing demand for my books, and I loved the freedom to be more generous.

My sole focus became money. When you have been financially insecure in your lifetime, it is life-altering. It changes you forever whether you like it or not. When you struggle with money, you feel like a failure. You feel like it is your fault and somehow you must deserve to live like that. It makes you feel shame, especially in the culture of 'hustle and earn' we

have here in the United States. When you don't know how you will feed your family or keep the electricity on, it's easy to make financial security your definition of success.

As my career grew, that became my new definition. I left sweet Selma behind, along with the simple life I had once coveted so much. My self-published and publishing royalties kept rolling in. I qualified for the loan on the house at Whatif Acres and a business loan to build my studio and acquire book inventory.

And I wanted *more.*

Because of my past, it was easy for me to decide that a full bank account meant I had achieved ultimate success as a human being. I was making a lot of money and to me, that meant I was a good and successful person. That was my truth.

My truth and perspective was about to shift *drastically.*

I'm going to be completely transparent with you. As I write this in Spring 2023, I have almost no money in the bank. Yes, for real. I have a mountain of debt and my business account is almost empty. I have a few events coming up, but I'm not exactly sure how I am going to pay my bills this summer.

At the start of 2022, book demand slowed. My royalty checks started getting smaller—and it happened fast. In less than a year, I lost the majority of my income from my publisher–income that I'd been able to reliably count on for ten years. In less than one year most of my income was gone. Poof! Just like that. I kept expecting my royalties to go back up, but they did not.

My own self-publishing sales slowed down dramatically too. I knew I had to pivot, so I self-published a few more picture books, started working with someone to help me streamline my online store, and learned how to use Facebook ads. Unfortunately, the ads didn't work well enough or fast enough. They were also expensive. I got myself deeper in a financial hole. That school visit income that I didn't miss so much in 2020 during lock down, was now sorely missed.

My business income dried up so much that last summer, I had to stop paying the mortgage on our home and I could not help with any extra or unexpected bills. Three years before that, I'd proudly taken over paying the mortgage and my husband paid all our other personal expenses. Kevin had to start paying for all of our bills because I no longer had any money left after paying my business expenses each month.

I know the fact that my husband and I have separate finances might seem confusing to some. I will explain this in more depth in a later chapter, but how we both treat and think of money began to contribute to problems in our marriage too.

I began to worry every minute of every day about money. How I could make more of it, how I could pay down debt. It was all I could think about. I woke up filled with anxiety and went to bed trying to figure out what to do. I had some very dark and scary moments during many a sleepless night wondering if I even deserved to be here any more with the financial mess I had created. I had an insurance policy. Let's just say it got *really* dark in my brain.

The more I focused on money and the less I focused on joy, the less I had of both.

Until last year, I had not had money issues in thirteen years. After losing a majority of my income in one year and racking up a mountain of debt, it has not been easy to remember that my worth as a human is not attached to my bank account.

It's easy to be joyful and see all the magic in the world when you have no money problems. Having money makes everything easier. It just does. It's a lie to say otherwise.

Once I began making money with my career, I loved to be generous with it. Money made me feel like I was a good person because I could do good things with it. Having money became my identity.

Do you see the problem I created for myself? If having money meant I was a success, if money meant I was a good person, what if my money went away? Then it *did*.

Who was I without money? This became the question I needed to answer this past year. It seems simple, but it was not an easy answer for me to find. I had tied my self-worth to my bank account, and that is a big mistake to make.

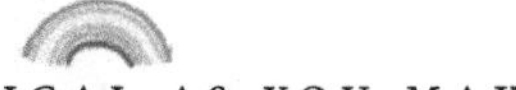

Our purpose in life is not to make a pile of money.

I want you to really hear that, read that, let that sink into your soul. *Our purpose in life is not to make a pile of money.*

I have come to understand that we are on this earth to have fun, to experience life and emotions, to love and to be loved, and to notice how truly magical it is to be alive.

How did I come to this understanding? How did I come to remember who I am in this life? *By taking my own advice.* By remembering the words that I have told children for over ten years, in forty-three states, in over one thousand schools.

I had forgotten. I had stopped living my own words. I had changed my priorities. I had lost my joy. Money made me forget who I really am.

The less money I made, the more I started to feel like a failure. I felt like I was letting down my husband, my family, my friends, and even strangers. I had so intertwined making money with who I was as a person that when sales were down, I felt like a failure as a human being. I felt like I had gone back in time to being that young mother who could not afford to feed her children.

It affected everything: my marriage, my self-worth, my outlook on life. That's how I got to that dark, joyless place.

I was back down at the bottom of that deep hole, and I was scared. I was consumed by thoughts of debt and making money. I was inundated on social media with "experts" trying to sell me some new system to help me make more money. I was getting more miserable with each passing day. Nothing was working—and then more tragedy struck.

My beloved rescue dog, Cornflake, suddenly declined in health. He had always had skin and allergy issues, but this was different. We finally found out he had an incurable autoimmune disease. We spent a large amount of money trying to find a way to slow the progression. I felt guilty because I had no money to contribute, and my husband had to take on even more financial responsibilities. Cornflake was worth every penny, though. He was the epitome of joy and love. Waking up with Cornflake was like waking up with sunshine. He lived each day with such happiness, even on the days he was in pain. Losing him when I was at my lowest put me into an even darker place.

I didn't think things could get worse. Then they *did.*

The week we realized that we needed to choose a merciful end for our sweet Cornflake, my world was shattered. A tragedy happened and we lost a family member.

When that happened, nothing mattered but my people. I dropped everything. I took care of my children and others who needed my help. This terrible situation prioritized everything for me. I realized I had felt worthless because I had equated my worth as a human being with my financial worth. And that was not true at all.

When this life-altering, heart-breaking, soul-shattering event happened, money didn't matter. My people mattered. In an instant I remembered who I was, and I realized I did not recognize who I had become. I was now someone filled with anxiety, going through the motions, valuing money over my mental health. I had lost myself. I had lost my joy.

When I was able to take care of my children, help them through this event, and be the light they needed me to be in the darkness, something in me broke free. I began to remember who I was again. In the midst of pain and despair, I also found joy again. I found joy in being there for my people. I began thinking about what I said at schools to children for over ten years. I realized those were the words I needed to tell myself again.

Before I begin each school presentation, I say a mantra. "Please let me have the words that need to be said, exactly how they need to be said, for exactly who needs to hear them. Let me be a vessel of light, love, and connection."

When I talk with an audience, there's an indescribable energy that flows back and forth between us. It feels electric, otherworldly—magical. We all feel it. I've had children raise their hands just to blurt out that they love me or to tell me that their heart feels like it's exploding out of their chest because they're so happy. Even the teachers come up to me to say the same types of things. We all feel the joy and the magic.

I realized I needed to create a book based on my school visit presentation. As I began to write this book, the one you are reading, I felt my joy returning. As I remembered the past twenty years of my life and the years before that, I began to feel lighter. My heart began to shine again.

This book is to remind you that your value has absolutely nothing to do with what your life might look like. It has nothing to do with your bank account, your profession, your title, the type of car you drive, or the type of home you have. I want you to consider what beliefs you have created for yourself that might not be true.

Who you are comes from a place deep inside of you. This book is to help you wake up your heart and soul and remember who you're meant to be.

I hope the words on the following pages help you to love who you get to be in this world, starting right now. You are spectacular. You don't have to do anything to earn your self-love. You can simply choose to believe you are worthy exactly as you are.

It's inevitable that I will be shattered again because that's what living as a human being means. But then I'll be able to reread the words I've written to myself, and to you, dear Reader.

When the darkness and doubt come back again, this book will help us remember that it always gets good again.

Your light may dim at times, sometimes even feel like it went out. But I promise you, it's still there inside you, waiting to shine again. Your light can *always* shine brightly again.

The rest of this book, starting with the next chapter, is an extended version of my school visit presentation. I've expanded on certain topics and added details I don't normally include due to the limited time I have with children at schools.

I hope you enjoy it. I definitely enjoyed writing it.

"Owning our story and loving ourselves through that process is the bravest thing that we will ever do."

-Brené Brown

4

How It Began

I HAVE THE BEST JOB in the whole wide world. Well, at least I think I do. I get to make up stories in my imagination, write them down, and then paint pictures about them. My life is magical. I am a children's book author and illustrator. I get to help others see the magic in themselves through my books.

As I tell you my story, I want you to believe with everything in you that you are supposed to have a magical life too. No matter what you might want to do with your life, who you might want to be, or who you already are, your life is supposed to feel amazing and awesome and even magical some days—just by being you.

I want to tell you the story of how I got to have my magical life. How I got to be sitting here, right now, writing this book for you.

To tell you my story, I'm going to have to bring you back to a long, long, looooong time ago when I was only four years old.

When I was four, I was a curious, mischievous kid. I used to get in trouble all the time, and my middle name got used a lot. I had a hard time obeying rules, and I didn't like people telling me what to do. Come to think of it, I still don't. Some things never change, right?

This one night was no different. I was supposed to be sleeping, but I wasn't sleeping. I was sneaking down the hallway. You see, at the end of the hallway, there was a closet. It wasn't just any closet. To the mind of a curious four-year-old, it was like a treasure closet. There were so many fun things to look at! Years later, I realized it was just a junk closet with all the miscellaneous items in our house that had no other place to go.

But this particular night, all I saw were treasures, like an old tape recorder with buttons to press or pink plastic curlers to run my fingers over. Then I saw a box on the back of the shelf. I needed to know what was in that box, so I grabbed it and hurried back to my bedroom.

I got down on the floor and opened the box. In it, I found paper, pencils, and erasers. But they didn't seem ordinary. They all seemed special. The pencils had no erasers on the ends. The gray eraser was soft and gummy. And the bright white paper? It was dreamy. I ran my little four-year-old fingers over the paper, feeling the texture of it. Slightly rough. It would be years later before I learned the term "tooth" for drawing paper, but feeling the tooth of that paper sparked something inside of me. That was the first moment I can consciously remember feeling joy.

That drawing paper sparked a joy in me that has never left.

I started looking through the thick sheets of stacked paper. That's when I saw them—drawings my mom had done. These drawings were amazing. They looked three-dimensional, but I could tell my mom had made them with just a pencil and an eraser. One of the drawings was of an old Indian chief with a huge feather headdress. I remember looking at his wrinkles. They looked like I should be able to touch them and feel the crevices in his tan, leathery skin.

The other drawing was of a little girl standing on a hill in the wind. I touched the flat paper, swearing I would feel fabric. It seemed impossible that I couldn't feel her billowing dress because it looked so real. Those two drawings made me understand that magic existed in my world. A whole world that looked like you could walk right into it could exist on a flat piece of paper.

It was also the first moment I could hear my heart speaking to me.

"Michelle, one day you're going to be an artist too. You will be able to draw like that one day," my heart whispered.

With everything in my four-year-old self, I knew that was true. *I was an artist.* But I also knew I was not waiting for someday. I needed to learn how to draw like that *now.*

*"Find joy in everything you
choose to do. Every job,
relationship, home . . . it's your
responsibility to love it,
or change it."*

-Chuck Palahniuk

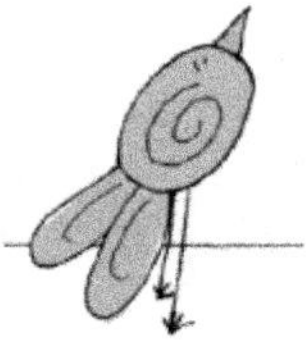

5

An Artist is Born

I STARTED PRACTICING THAT NIGHT. I looked at my mom's drawings, and I tried to copy them. Over and over and over I tried to copy the Indian chief and the little girl on the hill. I drew and drew and drew. I drew until I had used up every single sheet of that good drawing paper.

I didn't want to get into trouble, so I took everything and hid it under my bed.

A few days later I heard a familiar call from my mom, with a tone that let me know she was annoyed.

"Michelle Lee, come here please," my mom called from the dining room. She had used my middle name. Yep, I was in trouble.

"Yes?" I called as I came out of my bedroom.

"Did you take something that wasn't yours?" she asked.

I was never one to admit anything until I had to. “Like what?” I asked, trying to understand how serious a situation this was. I was also known to steal treats from the pantry before dinner; I needed to gather more information.

“Something out of the hall closet?” she asked with an eyebrow raised. My mom is no fool. I knew I was caught, but hey, I had two sisters, there was plausible deniability.

“No!” I said confidently.

“Michelle...” she said with a sternness that indicated she was not playing.

“Um, I used your paper to draw,” I finally admitted.

“Oh Michelle, you wasted all my good drawing paper?” She sighed loudly.

Now *I* was annoyed. “I didn’t *waste* it!” I ran to my room, retrieved my mom’s drawing supplies, and handed them over.

I watched as she went through all the smeared drawings where I had tried to rub the pencil to make light and dark tones like hers. She stayed quiet as she looked.

Finally she stood up and said, "Get on your shoes. Let's go."

Caught in my lie, I knew I'd better just be quiet and do as she said. I got on my shoes, and she grabbed her purse and car keys. I thought she was taking me to kid jail or something.

All she said was, "Get in the car."

Did they make jails for kids? I wondered. *It was just some paper. Was I really in this much trouble?*

But my mom didn't drive me to kid jail. She drove me to the most magical place in the whole wide world.

Now I know what you're thinking: she took me to *K-mart! (Target stands on the shoulders of giants, my younger readers!)*

Nope, she took me to a place even more magical than K-mart or Target combined. She took me to the art store. When I walked into that little mom-and-pop art store, it changed my life. If I close my eyes right now, I can smell that art store. I can smell paper, erasers, paint, and canvas. I can smell creativity in its rawest form.

My mother bought me my own paper, my own pencils, my own erasers, and my own special box to put it all in. That was it. All I ever wanted to do was draw. For birthdays, Christmas, Easter, all I ever asked for was art supplies.

I love to draw more than anything else in the world. I discovered a kind of magic happened when I drew as a child. It's a magic that still happens to this day.

When I draw, I'm not lonely. When I draw, I'm not worried about if people like me. When I draw, I'm not worried about marketing, or bills, or anything. When I draw, I go into another world where I am completely in the moment.

Drawing is joyful. How lucky was I that I found that joy at such an early age?

Do you have anything like that in your life? If not, did you ever? What gave you joy as a child that you might have stopped doing because of bills, or worry, or...life?

Can you get it back into your life? I bet you can. If you don't have anything like that in your life, what new thing can you try? I took

up the ukulele at 47! It's one of my biggest stress-relievers and I think the ukulele is one of the most joyful little instruments there is! I heartily recommend learning to play it if you need an idea for a new hobby! If I can learn it, *anyone* can–trust me.

Start thinking about how you can bring back a childhood joy or incorporate a new one into your life. You won't regret it.

"You're braver than you believe,
stronger than you seem, and
smarter than you think."
-A.A. Milne

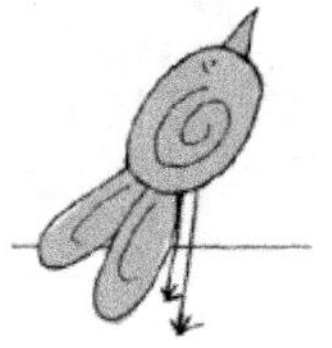

6

The ShowStopper

ALL THROUGH ELEMENTARY SCHOOL, I drew and drew and drew. All through middle school, I drew and drew and drew. But then in high school, I had an art teacher who taught me how to paint. I couldn't believe I loved painting even *more* than I loved drawing.

I first learned how to use oil paint. I found out I was very gifted at mixing colors. I could just look at a color on a page or in my mind, and I knew the exact ratio of colors to mix on my palette. My high school art classroom was my favorite place to be. I painted and painted and painted all the way through high school.

When I was sixteen, my mother was obsessed with Great Danes. After many months of this obsession, she tracked down a thirteen-month-old Great Dane who needed a home. His name was Dino. He was the sweetest, most enormous puppy ever. However, at the time we had a grumpy little dog named Muffin. Muffin was about fifteen years old and was *not* having Dino take over his house. He would viciously attack Dino's ankles. While Dino was never aggressive to Muffin, our little dog never stopped trying to attack. He was too old and set in his ways. Muffin was our beloved childhood dog, so my mom had to send Dino back.

My mother was heartbroken. One day, I was in art class deciding what to paint next. I was flipping through a magazine looking for inspiration, and I came across an advertisement that featured a giant face of a Great Dane. I knew exactly what to do.

We built our own canvases in art class. I wanted this to be a huge painting. I put together a 3 x 4 foot frame, stretched it with canvas, primed it with gesso, and started to paint my mom a giant Great Dane face. I spent the last three months of the school year working on it during class.

I was a junior that year and had found out we were moving from New Jersey to Texas for my senior year. I was devastated to have to move before my last year of high school. I adored my friends, and the thought of leaving my beloved art teacher devastated me. Ms. Dunn was instrumental in helping me learn who I was. As she put together a huge tub and filled it with tube after tube of oil paint to take to Texas, she said, "You know, you are good enough to do this for a living. Don't ever forget that."

I never forgot her words. They meant everything to me.

I finished the Great Dane painting later that summer and gave it to my mom. People would walk into our house and see this gigantic painting of a Great Dane. They'd ask if we had one and then look at us funny when we said we didn't. Thinking back, I guess it was odd to have a giant face of a Great Dane in your living room and no Great Dane to go with it. But it was eye-catching, and people loved it.

I bring several pieces of small and large canvas art with me to school visit presentations instead of PowerPoints. I assemble them in my hotel room at the beginning of the week and break them down and put them into a travelling golf bag to go on the plane at the end of the week. When teachers and librarians ask me if PowerPoint isn't easier than lugging giant paintings across the country, I just say, "Wait. You'll see why."

There is a part in my presentation where I show the children the Great Dane painting. I ask the children if they want to see something I painted in high school. Then, I dramatically turn that giant painting around.

Every time I reveal the Great Dane painting at a school, the children are astonished. They gasp with such joy and sometimes erupt in thunderous applause. It's easily my favorite moment.

I catch the attention of older, sometimes disinterested, fifth graders and teachers whose faces say, *Another presentation I need to attend? Ugh.* They all lean forward. They all wonder what other art I'll be showing as I continue.

Throughout my school visit years, I have made a handful of my book illustrations into extra-large canvases as well. As I read my books, I strategically turn them around throughout the presentation. Giant art is a showstopper. Giant art is also how I keep five-year-olds entranced for forty-five minutes straight. The Great Dane is my hook that grabs their attention; my other art and stories keep them rapt.

Thank you, sixteen-year-old Michelle, for painting a giant dog face.

"Not till we are lost ... do we begin to find ourselves."

-Henry David Thoreau

7

Old Toenails and Art School

WHEN WE GET DONE with high school, we can go to colleges, universities, vocational schools, or trade schools to learn about the things we love and hopefully how to make a living from them.

I bet you're thinking, *Obviously, Michelle wanted to go to art school.* And you're right.

But that is far from what I did. I went to school for physics and math.

I bet you're thinking, *Huh?*

Yeah, I know. Let me explain.

I was one of those kids for whom math and science came easily. I just was good at it. Or maybe I just had a good memory, I don't know. But when I took physics in high school, something just clicked. I really liked it. I was

good at it. It made me curious in a way no other subject had before, even art.

When it was time to pick a major for college, I chose art at first. But then my father said something to me that made a lot of sense and made me change my mind.

"Michelle," he said, "if you go to school for art, you'll be an artist. But if you go to school for science, you'll be a scientist and an artist because you're already an artist. Why don't you get an education so that you can be both?"

That made a lot of sense to me. So off I went to college as a physics major. I liked it. I liked it a lot. But I didn't love it. In the middle of my junior year, I just was not feeling what my classmates seemed to be feeling. As the course work became harder and harder, I just found myself with no desire to keep up with it. I was confused and not sure what was happening. I had always been a high achiever, but now I found myself not caring about the subject matter or my test scores. I was no longer competitive with my classmates. I just didn't care.

I felt lost.

That's when my heart spoke to me again, as clearly as it had when I was four years old.

Michelle, this is the rest of your life. Can you do this for the rest of your life? my heart whispered.

I knew the answer, but I was reluctant to do anything about it. I was midway through my junior year of college and had a 3.8 GPA. Did I really want to change everything? Did I really want to tell my parents that I had made a mistake and spent so much of their money on the wrong major?

The answer was a resounding *no.* I did not want to tell them any of that, so I didn't.

I didn't tell my parents I was dropping out of college. I withdrew from all my courses, sublet my apartment, and drove home from college in the middle of the night. I snuck into my parents' dark house and went up to my bedroom.

The next morning, I surprised my parents with an announcement. "I dropped out of college, and it's too late to do anything about it. I don't know what to do. I just need a minute to figure it out."

As you can imagine, that went over like a lead balloon. My parents were not happy with me at all. However, there was not much they could do except tell me I had to get a job while I figured things out. (As a parent now, I had no clue what I had put my parents through at the time. I sometimes *still* tell them I'm sorry about how I handled that.)

Here's the thing: I now knew exactly what I wanted to do. I wanted to go to art school, but I was too scared to tell them. I was also exhausted from spending three years working toward a degree in something that I knew wasn't going to fulfill me.

I wonder why we put so much pressure on seventeen- and eighteen-year-olds to know what they want to do for the rest of their lives? Why can't we let our young adults have a minute? Why can't we normalize not knowing, exploring, wondering, and wandering a bit until we begin to understand who we are? It's so much pressure to get it right. How many of us get it wrong and end up years down a path we might never have gone down if we had just had a moment to just...be?

I ended up getting a job as an assistant at a podiatrist's office thanks to one of my mom's friends. The office mostly catered to elderly people who needed toenail trims. It was a strange string of events that led me to helping trim elderly toenails and to a delightful 80-year-old coworker named Ethel.

One day, Ethel said something to me that changed my world.

"What the hell is a twenty-year-old doing here helping to clip old toenails?" Ethel asked me one day.

"It's interesting. Maybe I want to be a podiatrist," I said.

"That's a load of bull. What do you love?" she asked.

"Art," I replied immediately.

"Then why the hell are you here and not at art school?" she asked.

"I don't want to disappoint my parents," I replied.

"Look, let me tell you something. I got into Julliard. I wanted to be a concert pianist. My parents didn't think that was a career choice. Instead, I went into the military. I liked it. I met my husband. I had children. I had a good life. But guess what? It wasn't the life I was supposed to have. Don't let anyone stop you from living the life *you* want. Not even your parents. You only get one life. It belongs to you and no one else. Do what you want," she said.

Over the next several weeks, I applied to an art program, got in, quit my job, and told my parents I was going to art school.

The morning of the first day of art school my father said, "I think you're making the biggest mistake of your life."

That devastated me. It also gave me a resolve I'd never felt before. When I walked into my art school later that morning, I felt a rightness in my soul like I'd never felt before.

The road wasn't easy, as most roads worth travelling aren't. I had to work three jobs to afford to go there. I didn't sleep much at all, but I loved every second of it. Sometimes you're lucky enough to find out how hard you're willing to work for the things that you want. Never be scared of how hard it might be.

Old Toenails and Art School

"Sometimes things have to go wrong in order to go right."

-Sherrilyn Kenyon

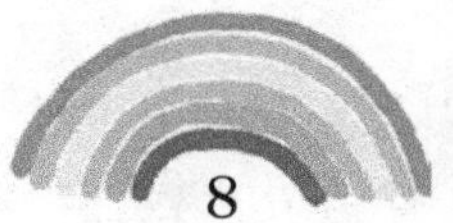

8

The Deep Darkness

I GRADUATED FROM THE ART Institute of Dallas with an associate degree in visual communications with an emphasis on graphic design. I also graduated seven months pregnant with my boyfriend's baby. A boyfriend my parents hated. How's that for choices that make your life easier?

I had gone from a straight A high school student that was going to get a PhD in physics, to an art college graduate that didn't even have a bachelor's degree. I was also about to be a twenty-three-year-old mother with no job with a partner who had no job either. My boyfriend also was a new graduate from the photography program. We had met the first day of art school.

I bet you can just imagine my parents' beaming pride.

I had made my life about as difficult as possible. I had dug myself into a really deep hole, but I was determined to prove I had not made a mistake by choosing a career in art.

The good thing about graduating pregnant is that no one will hire you. That was a blessing because that's how I realized I loved freelancing and being an entrepreneur. It was ridiculously hard, but I figured out how to make money without a conventional job.

Right after our son, Noah was born, my parents helped us to move from Dallas, Texas to Atlanta, Georgia. It was only four hours from my parent's home in Charlotte, NC. In Dallas we were 12 hours away from any family, so four hours was much better. We chose Atlanta for no other reason except it seemed like a fun city and my boyfriend had a connection to a photographer who said he would hire him for freelance work. Not exactly a stellar life plan, but we were young, optimistic parents in our twenties. You don't always make smart choices at that stage of life, right?

Being a young entrepreneur is hard. Being a young mom in a troubled marriage is harder than anything I could have imagined.

We got married when Noah was almost a year old. Not long after, I realized I had married a man who didn't seem to want to work for his family. Instead, he preferred to play video games or watch questionable material on the Internet for hours on end. He was verbally and emotionally abusive. I didn't want to admit I had made a mistake marrying him, so I kept most of that a secret for a long time. I decided if I just worked hard enough, I could fix everything.

Things were desperate money-wise. They became even worse when I realized I was unexpectedly pregnant a second time with our daughter, Sophia. I was thrilled because I loved being a mother, but I also knew we had no business bringing another life into this world when we could hardly take care of our first child financially.

We had to use food stamps to get by, and thank goodness the state of Georgia had a free healthcare program for children. I remember one time I needed to buy a medicated diaper

ointment for my son. The doctor said it was over-the-counter and easy to get. I knew I was in trouble. A prescription would have been free. Over-the-counter meant I needed to pay for it.

I only had ten dollars at the time. On the way home I stopped by a Winn-Dixie. I saw the ointment I needed. It cost $11.99. I didn't have enough money. I'm not proud of this, but I slipped the ointment out of the little box, slid it under my son in his car seat, and walked out of the store. I still feel so much shame to this day about that theft. It was one of my lowest points.

Our utilities were regularly getting turned off. I remember one time I got a check for a freelance gig on a Friday afternoon and then our electricity got turned off. I had no gas money, so I walked two miles to the bank to deposit the check (this was before cell phones) and then walked to the electric company to write a check that I hoped wouldn't bounce. When I got home at least the electricity had come back on.

I want to take a moment to remind all of us that many of us are one accident, one bad decision, one unexpected job loss, or illness away from living a life we never thought we'd be living. The next time you see someone use food stamps, or perhaps hear about a theft on the news, I beg you to consider that desperate people do desperate things sometimes. Not because they want to, but because sometimes, they just don't see any other way. *Assume the best about people whenever you can—especially when you have no idea what their story is.*

I was in a terrible marriage. I could hardly pay my bills and I could hardly take care of my children. I could not believe this had become my life.

Maybe my father had been right. Had I made the biggest mistake of my life?

Then a single moment changed everything for me.

"I get by with a little help from my friends."

-The Beatles

9

Chalk-drawn Dreams

Ironically, I loved being a mother more than anything else in this world. I say ironically because the last thing I ever wanted to be was a mother. I hated babysitting as a teenager and often said, "You couldn't ever pay me enough money to entertain small children."

I could not have predicted how much I adored being a mother, even though we were poor. I found every inexpensive way to entertain my children. I took them to parks and free events, and I made art for them. One time my son wanted stars in his bedroom. I didn't have money for store-bought decals or stickers, so I cut stars out of cardboard, wrapped them in tin foil, and hung them in the corner of his room. He loved them.

I painted murals on their walls and constantly drew pictures with them. Another inexpensive thing I did with my children was draw with chalk on the sidewalks outside.

That's what we were doing on a beautiful summer evening in August of 2002. We were living in an apartment complex that had sidewalks that crisscrossed across a large green space. There were a lot of kids in the complex, and I used to take a big bucket of chalk outside so we could all draw on the sidewalks.

On this summer evening, colored pieces of chalk were scattered everywhere, and my children and all the neighbor children were drawing. I happened to pick up a yellow piece of chalk. At the time, we had a yellow Labrador named Lucy. I decided to draw a picture of Lucy.

When I was done, a little girl walked by and said, "That's really good, you should draw for a living."

Wouldn't that be amazing, I thought to myself.

I looked at that little drawing on the sidewalk, and something shifted. It felt like sunshine had filled up inside of me. I felt a kind of joy I had not felt in a long time.

That's what you're supposed to be doing, Michelle. That's it, my heart whispered.

I really had no idea what that was supposed to mean. It was just a silly little dog drawing on the sidewalk. I couldn't stop thinking about it though. Later that night as I was making dinner and then as I was putting my kids to bed, that chalk outline kept dancing around in my brain. I could not shake the feeling that I needed to do something about it.

It had been a long time since I had painted. I didn't even have any art supplies. Art supplies are expensive. There was no way to justify such a luxury when I barely had money for food.

Still, I found myself in a Big Lots the next day. Did you know Big Lots has an art aisle? I didn't either. I bought a cheap 16 x 20 inch canvas, some cheap tubes of acrylic paint, and cheap paint brushes. The guilt of using money for any of this was overwhelming, but the feeling that I needed to paint that little dog outline was more overwhelming.

That night, after putting my kids to bed, I turned that little chalk outline of my dog into a painting. When I finished the painting, the feeling of joy was overwhelming. I honestly felt like I was vibrating with joy and love when I looked at it. I never wanted that feeling to go away, so I hung the painting up where I could see it all the time.

Then something happened. I painted and gifted a pet portrait to Drew, a good friend of mine back in Dallas. I was with him years ago, when he saw an adorable Dalmatian puppy for adoption in a store parking lot. He was smitten with her. He adopted the puppy and named her Pepper. Pepper was the light of his life and I loved gifting him a painting of the now fully-grown, Pepper. He was delighted with my fun cartoonish style and encouraged me to paint more like that and sell them. That's all anyone really needs, isn't it? A bit of encouragement and to be told we are good at something? Drew and Pepper had a huge impact on what happened next in my life.

That's when my entrepreneurial spirit took over. I cobbled some money together for more canvases and began painting all types of dogs.

I found an art festival with an entry fee I could afford and borrowed a cheap sun tent from my sister.

I was going to sell my art! I knew this was it. This was the answer I was looking for.

My mom and older sister, Jennifer, came in for the art festival and helped me set up my booth. I hung up my colorful, cheerful dog art and waited for people to buy it. But no one did. People smiled and said how much they loved my art, but no one bought anything.

I was devastated. I had wasted so much money on this. I felt foolish and dejected until someone walked into my tent with a Boston Terrier on a leash. She looked around and said, "Do you have any Boston Terrier art?"

That was my lightbulb moment. I replied, "No, but I can take a photo of your dog and do a custom portrait for you."

She was delighted and put down a deposit for a 16 x 20 inch painting of her dog. I was thrilled.

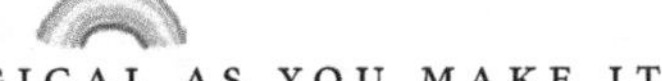

I quickly grabbed a blank canvas and painted a sign to hang up. It said "Don't see your dog? Get a custom pet portrait!"

It worked like a charm! People started coming in with their dogs and ordering pet portraits. I took photos, or they agreed to send me photos.

I realized too late that I had priced my custom pet portraits too low, but I honestly didn't care. People were buying my art! I was beyond thrilled. I got seventy commissions that October weekend. I was in heaven.

I also promised every single person that the portrait would be done in time for Christmas. In my excitement, I promised to paint and deliver seventy paintings in six weeks.

Did I mention I had just started a new full-time graphic design job? Plus I had two children in elementary school? And I was in a bad marriage?

However, when the universe finally gives you something you've wanted your whole life, you don't complain. You just do it.

I woke up early to paint. I stayed up late to paint. I painted every minute of the weekend. It almost killed me, but I delivered the last pet portrait—of a rabbit named Jack—on Christmas Eve at a Starbucks in town.

My husband at the time loved the extra money, but complained I was obsessed with this new side career. I felt like I couldn't figure him out. If I made more money it was great, but I better not give him less attention. My confidence was building, but my marriage was breaking down.

Even with our marriage troubles, I was proud of myself. I had done it. I had delivered every painting and kept my word. For the first Christmas in years, we had some extra money in the bank.

I am still good friends with Drew. He has a lovely wife, Melissa, and the most adorable son Ollie. They live in Colorado now and stayed with us at Whatif Acres when they were visiting Florida a few years ago. Drew still encourages me all the time. Friends like that are priceless, never take them for granted.

I have to tell you another crazy side story right here. During the first year of painting pet portraits, I advertised them by hanging fliers in coffee shops. It was free and got me a lot of commissions. One time, I got a commission from a man who saw my flier, and called me to request a portrait of their dog as a surprise for his wife's birthday.

Because it was a surprise, when it was done, he asked me to deliver it to his work. I dropped it off to him and he was thrilled with it. A coworker of his happened to see the pet portrait in his cubicle later that day. His coworker asked for my contact information to inquire about a pet portrait of his dog.

The man emailed me and asked if I could do a pet portrait of Skylar, a German Shepherd puppy he and his wife had just gotten a few weeks earlier. I responded back that German Shepherd's markings change a lot as they grow and it would be better to wait a few months before I painted her. He agreed and promised he would email me later, but he never did.

However, I would eventually paint that pet portrait Skylar. I painted her portrait when she became my dog too.

In a crazy, cosmic (dare I say magical?) set of circumstances, my future husband, emailed me about a ordering a pet portrait before we ever knew each other and were both married to other people.

Years later, then both single, we met through the dating service, Yahoo Personals. We started chatting and made the connection.

Crazy, right?

"Bravery is the audacity to be unhindered by failures, and to walk with freedom, strength, and hope, in the face of things unknown."

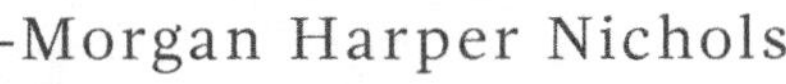

-Morgan Harper Nichols

10

Big Brave Questions

FOR YEARS I PAINTED pet portraits part-time while I kept a full-time graphic design job. I would set up booths at local art festivals throughout the year. I painted at night and on weekends.

After the first year and a half of doing this, I finally had enough confidence to end my marriage. I'm grateful for the generosity of my parents, who helped me financially during the divorce. I had debt and terrible credit. They had to co-sign a lease for me to get an apartment of my own and paid for my legal fees.

The divorce was long, ugly, and horrible. After two years of ugliness, I became a single mom of an eight-year-old and a six-year-old. Sometimes divorce is the only way, but I don't

wish it on anyone. Those were the two hardest years of my life.

During that time, I worked as a graphic designer at a community college and painted pet portraits in my spare time. That pet portrait money made all the difference in getting by. Plus, painting gave me a joy I clung to during those dark, difficult days.

I painted pet portraits for about eight years total. In those eight years, I painted over eight hundred pets for people all over the country. When hundreds of people begin telling you that you're good at something and they value what you do, two things happen.

First you get confident. You feel good about yourself. But next? That's when you get brave.

You get brave enough to ask yourself a big, brave question.

My big, brave question was this: *If I can have this amazing life where people buy my art—what if? What if I could have more? What if I could have my magical dream life? The one I have secretly wanted since I was eight years old?*

What if?

"The two most important days in life are the day you're born and the day you find out why."

-Mark Twain

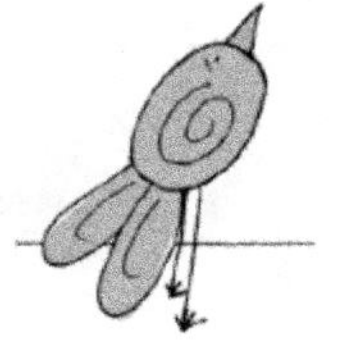

11

The Audacity to Want More

When I was in second grade, our school librarian read *Strega Nona* by Tomie dePaola to my class. I was rapt with attention. I loved having picture books read to me. After a few pages, I raised my hand and asked, “Where do those pictures come from?”

“Tomie drew them; he’s the illustrator,” my librarian answered. She continued reading the story.

After a few more pages, I raised my hand again. “Where did he get the story from?”

“He made it up. It’s his job. He’s the author too,” she said.

The librarian finished the book, but I didn’t hear another word. I was lost in my dreams.

That's a job? Some adults get to make up stories and draw pictures about their stories for a job? That sounded like the most magical life I could ever imagine.

In that moment, in that library, I realized who I was supposed to be in this world. I knew it with every ounce of my being. But I kept it a secret. I never told anyone. I never said it aloud. Not even in a college art class called Children's Book Illustration.

Want to know why?

As a child, I was scared. I was too scared of wanting something so much. I was too scared of having a dream so big. I was scared of taking up too much space, of being noticed.

Because what if I failed? What if I couldn't have it? What if others saw I wasn't good enough? That would hurt way too much. So I never told anyone.

Then as an adult, I think I decided I didn't deserve the life of my dreams. I ignored any feelings that there might be more for me in this life. I didn't deserve more than I had. I had made poor choice after poor choice since high school. I had made my life so difficult. I had no one to blame for the life I was living. I was divorced and honestly, money was just as scarce as when I was married. My life was hard and even worse? I had made my children's lives hard, confusing, and heart-breaking. Children get no say when their family gets dissolved right before their eyes. The guilt I felt over that was enormous. Who was I to think I deserved more with all the damage I had done?

Until one day, after painting enough pet portraits, I was finally confident enough, finally brave enough to have the audacity to say aloud to myself—and to the world—that I knew who I was meant to be.

I was going to be a children's picture book author and illustrator.

I deserved more.

*"If you really look closely,
most overnight successes
took a long time."*

-Steve Jobs

12

Ask, You Might Get an Answer

I GOT DOWN TO WORK. I began researching how to get published. I read everything I could find on the Internet and in print. I sat with books at the bookstore and took notes. Of course, I was too poor to buy any books, so I hid in corners, writing down notes about how to find and submit to publishers and agents.

I began working on picture book ideas. I was sketching, painting, and practicing every spare minute I had, all while working full time and painting pet portraits.

I finally decided I was ready to try to get a two-book deal. The books were called *Dogs, Dogs!* and *Cats, Cats!* They were fun, rhyming books inspired by all those pet portraits I had painted through the years.

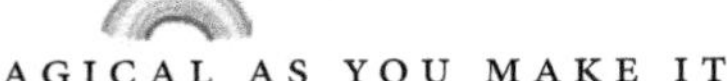

After enough research, I realized I needed to get an agent if I was going to be published with a big publisher. I began the process of submitting to literary agents to find representation.

Let me tell you, getting an agent and trying to get published is not easy. It takes tenacity and courage. You had better be prepared for rejection. A lot of rejection. Like, a *lot*.

I was about a year into my quest to find an agent, and I was getting pretty dejected. The rejections were coming fast and furious with little feedback. But one day, I got a nice, albeit quite fast rejection via email from Steven Malk at Writers House. I was defeated, but felt I had nothing to lose. So I responded to his rejection.

I asked him if there was something obviously wrong with my manuscripts that I was not seeing. I asked him to be brutally honest with me and tell me if I was wasting my time trying to get published.

To my surprise, he wrote back right away. "Your concepts are good. You rhyme well. However, I don't represent authors who rhyme because it makes translations very difficult to sell to other markets. Also, it's difficult to get a brand-new, unknown author and illustrator a book deal."

When I read that, I was happy that he had complimented my writing, but I also felt more hopeless than ever. I wrote back. "This seems hopeless. Do you have any advice at all to help me? I feel like this is what I'm meant to do."

His last response changed everything.

He wrote, "Go to the bookstore. Find a picture book by an author and illustrator that rhymes. Find out who represents them. Submit to that agent."

So obvious, right? But it would have never occurred to me in a million years to do that.

I thanked him profusely for his time and immediately went to the children's section at Barnes & Noble.

I scanned the shelves, pulling out any books that were written and illustrated by the same person. I sat at a tiny table meant for children and opened one book after another, looking to see which were written in rhyme.

Finally, I found the book *Llama Llama Red Pajama* by Anna Dewdney. I went home and

looked up her website. I found out she was represented by Deborah Warren with East West Literary Agency.

I looked up her submission guidelines and immediately emailed Deborah and sent her my two manuscripts for consideration. She emailed back right away and asked me to call her.

After an hour on the phone, she agreed to represent me.

Can you *believe* that? I *know.*

Mr. Malk could have never responded to my follow-up email. What if he was just too busy that day? But he wasn't. He answered me. His advice was what got me an agent just a few hours later.

I had learned a valuable lesson. Always, always, be willing to put yourself out there and ask for advice.

Because again, *what if*?

"Sometimes, you have to give up. Sometimes, knowing when to give up, when to try something else, is genius. Giving up doesn't mean stopping. Don't ever stop."

-Phil Knight

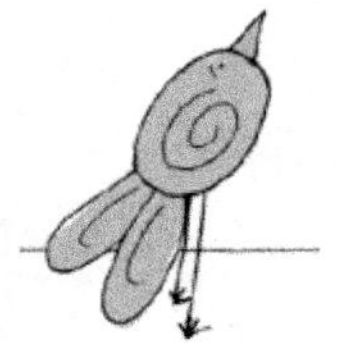

13

When Your Ship Sails On By

A GOOD AGENT IS WORTH their weight in gold. They have connections to all the big publishers. They make 15 percent of any deal they get you, and it is well deserved. They are amazing. They are the secret sauce.

What no one tells you is that agents also get you rejections at supersonic speed. If you find publishers that will accept submissions without an agent, it can take weeks or months to hear back. With an agent, you get your rejections fast. And boy did I get them.

When I got my agent, I was sure my ship had come in. *This is it,* I thought. *Here we go!* I had no idea how wrong I was.

Time went and went...and went. In fact, two more years went by. I got rejections every few days from my agent. She was on the west coast, and I was on the east. She would send out rejections at the end of her day, which meant I woke up to them. I finally asked her to send my rejections earlier in her day because starting my day with yet another rejection was getting too depressing.

All my rejections went a little something like this:

"We don't want a dog book."

"We don't want a cat book."

"We don't want a rhyming book."

"This just isn't for us."

Or various forms of the above. Then I finally got the rejection that did me in. They didn't care for my art style. They wrote, "Art too stagnant. Not right for children's picture books."

That was it. I was done. One person can only take so many rejections before something breaks inside of you. That last rejection was it for me. I couldn't take it anymore. After a combined three years of rejections, I'd had enough. I quit.

I told my agent to stop sending out my books to publishers. I told her I was done. My worst fear had happened. I had tried my hardest, and I had failed. I was not good enough.

It is a humbling thing when you realize you cannot have the thing you want most. I had risked being rejected and had gotten...rejected.

I was absolutely broken.

"There is always light.
If only we're brave enough
to see it. If only we're
brave enough to be it."

-Amanda Gorman

14

You Don't Always Get What You Want

I WAS NUMB FOR A while after I decided to give up on my dream of being a published children's book author and illustrator. I was 35 now and a few years out from my divorce. I got a full-time graphic design job. Having a paycheck that got deposited into my bank account every two weeks was exactly what I needed. I had started dating a nice man I liked a lot. He was sweet, reliable, and had an amazing work ethic. He was everything my ex-husband was not.

Quick note about my boyfriend. I almost would not date him because of his name. His name was Kevin and that was the name of my ex-husband. I could not handle that. We decided not to date and hung out as friends for about a year. We began turning down dates with others to hang out as friends, and finally realized we

very much wanted to be romantic partners. The Universe has a hilarious sense of humor. Kevin became my boyfriend, best friend, and ultimately my husband a few years later in September, 2009.

Meanwhile, I was tired of the roller coaster of rejection. I wanted to have a normal, predictable life. I wanted to date this wonderful man and not worry about dreams that I might or might not be able to accomplish.

I stopped painting pet portraits. I threw myself into my graphic design job and did normal mom things. Life became calm and peaceful.

Until the whisper in my heart started to come back. *Michelle, it's time. You know you can't quit. You know who you are.*

Nope. No way was I listening to that voice again. I had been duped enough. I was done. D-O-N-E.

I know it's hard. But you can't quit. The only way you can truly fail is to quit. Don't quit.

I ignored that tiny voice for as long as I could. I did not want to be rejected again. I did not want to feel like a failure. I hated not feeling good enough.

The whispers grew louder. I woke up to them. I went to sleep with them. Finally, I couldn't ignore them anymore.

I supposed I had finally rested enough. I had healed enough and perhaps toughened to rejection enough. I have learned there is nothing wrong with resting and taking breaks. As I've gotten older, I have learned to value resting more than I ever have. Yes, because I no longer have the stamina I did in my thirties, but also because I finally understood that rest is as necessary as action. Burning the candle at both ends not only uses you up faster, it also doesn't leave any space for the magic to happen. There is no space for The Universe, God, Source, or whatever it is you want to call it to help you. Sometimes, you need to rest and replenish and let go of the *how*. Trust in the magic and *know* that whatever or whomever you believe in, knows *how*.

Looking back, I know I didn't choose to rest, I thought I gave up on my dream. But as always, life was working for me in the background the whole time while I took that much-needed rest from years of rejection.

Fine. I'll ask my agent if she has any suggestions, I thought.

As if the universe itself knew it was the right time, my agent wrote to me that very day. She said there was an editor named Emma Dryden who just started her own company and was looking for new clients. She had been a vice president at Simon & Schuster. My agent said she normally would never suggest that a client pay for edits, but she felt like my rejections had a lot of promise to them. Maybe if we could just tweak my manuscripts a bit, we'd get a yes.

I contacted Emma. After reviewing my *Dogs, Dogs!* manuscript, she agreed to take me on as a client. It was pricey, but I knew she was worth it. Plus, I had to know I had tried everything I could to make my dream come true.

I was surprised when I got her edits back. They weren't major. She reflowed the order of my rhymes and created a better rhythm to the pages. She told me to finish the sketches in my dummy book, which is a mock-up of the book's pages. She said they were too rough. She told

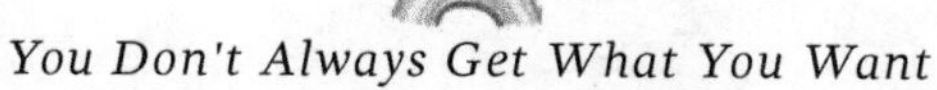

me to draw the page illustrations in detail so the editor could really envision what I wanted the book to look like.

Excitedly, I made all her edits and sent the polished manuscript to my agent. I felt a renewed sense of hope.

Maybe my dream wasn't dead.

"The universe is always conspiring to help us, if we only trust its wisdom."

-Ralph Waldo Emerson

15

Get Your Head Right

A FEW WEEKS LATER, I was on my way to Ronald McDonald House. I had started volunteering there a few months earlier. I usually painted for about an hour each Wednesday night with the siblings and parents of children who were in cancer treatments or receiving other medical treatments and procedures.

It was a Wednesday evening in August, and I was almost to Ronald McDonald House. Kevin called and said that a publisher had contacted him and asked him to write a book.

I must say, Kevin was, and still is the smartest man I've ever met. He's an expert in many things computer related but especially cyber security. At the time, he had already published a computer book. But being an author was not his job; nor did he want it to be.

"So they just called you? Out of the blue? A publisher? Asking you to write a book?" I asked.

"Yes," he answered.

"They offered you a contract?" I asked. I could feel my face getting hot.

"Yes," he said again.

Tears welled up in my eyes. It wasn't fair. I had been rejected for three years. I had worked so hard. And Kevin wasn't even *trying* to get a book published. It was infuriating.

"That's exciting. I'm really happy for you," I managed to choke out.

"Oh..." he said, finally realizing how it must have made me feel. "I'm sorry. I don't know what I was thinking. I was just excited and wanted to share. That was insensitive of me," he said.

I took a deep breath, assured him it was fine, and said we would celebrate when I got home later.

After we hung up, I parked and closed my eyes. I wanted to cry and feel sorry for myself. But when I opened my eyes, I saw the heart logo at the top of the building. I was about to go into a building where parents didn't know if their children would grow up. Where they didn't know if any of their children's hopes and dreams would come true because they weren't sure they'd even have a future.

Suck it up, Michelle. You have nothing to complain about. You have a good life, a husband you love and who loves you, and most importantly, you have two healthy children. Now go in there and help these kids and parents have some fun painting and help them forget about their fears for an hour.

I had gotten my priorities straight. I knew what was important. I felt a deep sense of knowing that my time would come.

I texted Kevin to say that I was okay and I really was incredibly happy for him. I chose to be inspired by his success instead of jealous. This shift from jealousy to inspiration was an important moment for me, especially because of what happened next.

I always left my phone in the car, so I would be mindfully present when I was painting with the families. I checked my emails one last time before going inside.

That was exactly the moment when I got this email from my agent with a response from Kane Miller Publishing's Editor, Kira Lynn:

****

Sent: Wednesday, August 25, 2010 1:01 PM
To: Deborah Warren
Subject: Re: EWAgency -- DOGS, DOGS submission

Okay, have to tell you - we REALLY like this! Any idea when CATS might be available?

****

Yes. That timing *really* happened. Crazy, right? *I know*!

I told my agent to reply that I needed to polish up *Cats, Cats!* and I'd get it to her the following Monday. Here's the thing. There was no *Cats, Cats!*. I had always said there was, but we had only ever sent out *Dogs, Dogs!* I had never gotten around to writing the companion book because my dog book had always been rejected before anyone ever asked to see the cat book. After a while, it just seemed silly to write the book if no one was ever going to ask to see it.

If you go back over a decade in my Facebook timeline, you will see a post from that Wednesday night. It reads something like "Calling all my friends with cats! Send me adjectives describing them! I can paint them, but I've never had any! Tell me what your cats are like!"

I took the next two days off work to write and sketch *Cats, Cats!*. Then I emailed Emma to see if she could do an emergency weekend edit of *Cats, Cats!*. Luckily, she generously agreed to do it with no extra rush fee. She had the edits back to me by Sunday afternoon, and my agent submitted *Cats, Cats!* the following Monday.

Eight days later, I received a two-book offer to be published by Kane Miller.

I had done it. I had made my big, giant dream a reality.

*"We do not create our destiny;
we participate in its unfolding.
Synchronicity works as a
catalyst toward the working
out of that destiny."*

-David Richo

16

Synchronicity

THEN ANOTHER BIT OF magic proved this was all happening exactly as it should. Shortly after I signed my book contract with Kane Miller, I was perusing their online catalog. I wasn't familiar with the company and wanted to see what other books they had published. I laughed when I realized they had published the wildly popular title *Everybody Poops*. But as I scrolled further, my jaw dropped.

It could not be. No way.

There on the screen was the book. *Selma*.

My purse was hanging on the back of my chair. I reached in without ever taking my eyes off the computer screen. I pulled out the little red book I had carried around with me ever since I had bought it years ago. I turned it over. There it was. The logo of Kane Miller. The same company who would now be publishing my first two books. How crazy is *that*?

Unbeknownst to me at the time, Kane Miller had just been acquired by EDC Publishing. They had a huge direct sales division. Imagine Mary Kay or Tupperware, but with children's books. The direct sales division was called Usborne Books & More, now known as PaperPie. They had, and still have, thousands of women (and a few men) who sell books across the country directly to parents, schools, and libraries.

I had always wanted to do school visits, and these women had relationships in schools across the country. I could not believe my luck! It was as if all those rejections had happened so I could get my yes from the exact right publisher for me.

In June 2011, *Dogs, Dogs!* and *Cats, Cats!* were published. I began visiting schools to do presentations that fall. My dreams had come true. It was even better than I ever could have imagined.

I was booked solid that fall and the following spring. I traveled fifteen weeks out of the school year that first year. Because I shared custody with my ex-husband, I could do this. We lived close to each other, and we alternated custody each week. The weeks the kids stayed with their father, I traveled across the country to schools.

Now, I want to pause and really make sure you see what has happened in my life so far. I made my dreams come true. Not because I was extra lucky. Not because I was extra special. Not because I was better than anyone else. I created my magical dream life simply because I paid attention to the whispers from my heart and acted on them. These synchronicities are not by chance. This is the magic you will experience and see when you begin looking for it and trust your heart.

First when I was four years old, my heart told me I was an artist.

Then when I was eight years old, it told me I was an author and illustrator.

When I was in college, it made me understand I needed to go to art school.

As a young mother, it told me to draw that chalk outline of my dog, Lucy.

That whisper from my heart started my painting career, which gave me confidence and developed my art skills. Then I was finally brave enough to say aloud who I truly was.

I was meant to create books for children—and I made it happen.

As I began touring the country, I realized I was also meant to inspire children to listen to their hearts and follow their dreams. I wanted to teach children to learn to trust their hearts as soon as possible. I knew listening to your heart is how you find joy and achieve your dreams.

I want that for you too. So often, adults think it's too late for them. They think the time has passed; they have missed out on their dreams.

Are you one of those adults? It is never too late! You need to start listening to your heart. Right now. Today!

If you quiet the loud, negative voice of your brain, you will begin to hear the whispers in your heart. They are quiet. But if you get still, you will hear your heart asking you to find joy in your life. Joy is one of our main purposes in life.

We are meant as humans to be playful and joyful. We are meant to love and to be loved. We

were given bodies so we can experience things with them. So often we choose to listen to our brains instead of our hearts. Want to know which voice is which? If the voice is negative or makes you feel bad, it's your brain. If the voice makes you feel hopeful and sparks joy, it's your heart.

We have been trained to listen to the incessant negative thinking of our brains. Here is something that has really helped me. Thinking and thoughts are not the same. Thoughts can inspire. Thoughts can be a knowing. Thinking can ruin it all. Pay attention to thoughts, not to thinking. But always, always listen to thoughts that light you up inside—those are your heart talking.

"Success is not final, failure is not fatal: it is the courage to continue that counts."

-Winston Churchill

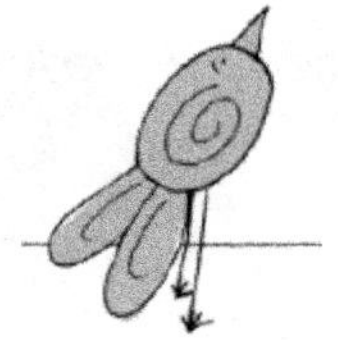

17
The Whatif Monster is Our Friend

HOW DO YOU FIND your joy?

That's simple. You have to do the things that make your heart feel like it is bursting with sunshine.

How do you find those things?

That answer is simple too, but you might not like the process very much.

You have to try new things. You have to mess up. You have to make mistakes. Sometimes you have to get hurt, maybe physically or emotionally—or both. Sometimes you are going to have to ask for help. Doing those things might make you mad, make you cry, and even make you feel like you want to quit.

Don't you dare quit. We can't quit. Because the tough times teach us who we are, how strong we are, how capable we are, and how much we deserve joy and magic.

We can take breaks. We can regroup. We can change course. But we cannot quit. I'm telling you the same thing I am telling myself right now: *Don't you dare quit.*

However, I know doing hard and scary things is, well, hard and scary. Which is why I wrote my next book for children–and you.

In 2012, I was inspired to write what would become my best-selling children's book *Jonathan James and the Whatif Monster.* I wanted to create a book that helps us to hear the tiny whispers in our hearts, which can be hard to hear over the roar of the insecurities our brain loves to remind us of again and again.

Here is the text from my book. You didn't know you were getting a free book in this book, did you? Because the text in this book is so simple yet so effective, I wanted to make sure you could read it here.

The Whatif Monster is Our Friend

Some Whatif Monsters like to hang out,
and fill up our heads with worry and doubt.

They are sneaky and quiet and quick as a blink,
the words that they whisper can change how we think.

Jonathan James heard those words full of dread,
and all those "what ifs" got stuck in his head.

What if you tumble? What if there's wind?
What if you slip, and your knee gets all skinned?

What if they giggle? What if it's chilly?
What if you jump and look really silly?

What if it's hard? What if you're bad?
What if they laugh and make you feel sad?

What if it's dark? What if it's scary?
What if there's something giant and hairy?

What if you lose? What if you're last?
What if you're slow and never get fast?

What if she laughs? What if she runs?
What if she thinks you're not any fun?

"Now wait just a minute! I have something to say,
after hearing 'what ifs' all through the day.

I hear all your worries; I hear all your claims.
But what if you're wrong?" asks Jonathan James.

What if I climb to the top of that tree,
and I never slip or skin up a knee?

And what if I jump right into that pool,
and everyone thinks I look really cool?

And what if baseball is nothing but fun,
and I end up hitting a triple home run?

And what if my drawing goes up on the wall,
and everyone thinks it's the best one of all?

And what if I taste some of that food,
and it puts my mouth in a really good mood?

And what if I run in a really big race,
and have a great time no matter what place?

And what if I sleep and have the best dream
that monsters are sweeter than they all seem?

And what if the chance I take in the end,
is just how I find my very best friend?

If you want to see the illustrations, you should totally buy this book. You won't regret it. It's on Amazon or on my website at MNScreative.com. Go ahead, I'll wait. Back? Great! I'll sign it for you if you bought it from me. But if you wanted the free shipping on Amazon, no worries. I get it. (I got my hardback rights to this book back this year, so I am 100% allowed to put this text into this book, in case you were wondering. And also why you should go check out the completely redesigned version of this book with bonus material at the end. How's that for a shameless plug?)

Jonathan James and the Whatif Monster celebrated ten years in print in 2022, and that's no small thing in today's publishing world. I have had emails, texts, phone calls, and letters telling me how this book has changed people's lives or their children's lives. To have a book, a monster, an idea, or anything that can help us to shift our thinking is such a valuable tool. I will never stop being grateful that the words to this book were gifted to me to share with others.

The Whatif Monster has come to be a secret weapon for all of us. I tell children (and adults) to make friends with your Whatif Monster. He loves to worry. In fact, I invented him to worry for us. When you can give him all your worries and what-ifs and clear them out of your mind, you know what's left over?

All the wonderful and good what-ifs!

Instead of *What if I fail?*, choose the thought, *What if I succeed?*

What if I'm terrible now becomes *What if I'm amazing?*

What if I can't transforms to *What if I can?*

This tiny shift in thought can, and will, change everything!

When you focus on all the good and wonderful what-ifs, they are so much more likely to happen. The power of our minds is greater than we realize. We believe what we tell ourselves. We can condition ourselves to say positive or negative things, so why not choose the positive? It takes practice, but it works.

Even if you try something and you are terrible, you can say to yourself, *What if I ask for help? What if I practice? What if I get better?* Yes, it's simple. Sometimes the simplest solutions are the best.

The only way you can fail is if you stop trying. You can rest. You can take breaks.

You can change your mind about what you want. You can change your perspective. You can ask for help. Just don't quit! Please don't quit on what your heart wants.

"Your need for acceptance can make you invisible in this world. Don't let anything stand in the way of the light that shines through this form. Risk being seen in all of your glory."

-Jim Carrey

18

Not Everyone Will Get You, Bob

LET ME TELL YOU something. When you start to quiet your brain and listen to the whispers in your heart, amazing, incredible, *magical* things begin happening in your life. Don't take my word for it. Begin. You'll see.

There is a shift you will feel when you begin to live your life for *you*. When you own who you are and who you want to be, the magic begins. It might be subtle at first, but it gets stronger each day when you realize you are living your truth and trusting that you are here on purpose, designed with exactly the right packaging, materials, and software. Even when you don't have yourself completely figured out, there is a shift deep inside your soul that will be saying, *Yes! You are figuring it out! There was never anything wrong with you at all.*

Life is hard and complicated and confusing for all of us. The thing that makes it all easier is trusting that we are not a mistake. We have been given this gift of living. The gift is the journey–the highs, the lows, the joys, the tears. Getting to take this journey unapologetically as yourself is what makes the sometimes unbearable weight of being human...bearable.

Once you begin accepting and loving the unique human being that you are, coincidences, luck, happy accidents, and chance meetings will begin to occur. You will meet someone who can help you with a challenge you weren't sure how you'd overcome. Or a friend will offer to babysit out of the blue so you can go do something you've decided will make you happy. Maybe a few extra dollars will show up for art supplies you swore you had no extra money for. This is not luck or coincidence. It is the universe working for you because you have finally aligned your mind with your heart. I think all of these amazing things have been there all along, but when we're ready, we finally begin to *see* them and *recognize* them. It happens like magic.

However, sometimes something else happens when you are following your heart and being true to yourself. That's why I wrote *Bob Is a Unicorn.*

In that book, my good friend Bob is totally a unicorn. But none of his friends seem to get it. They think he's silly or wasting their time. Bob asks his friends to play with him, but no one will. Dejected and feeling a little bit broken inside, Bob decides to quit and go home.

But Bob doesn't make it home, thank goodness. On his way home, Bob runs into a fairy. On this page, you see a watercolor illustration of a beautiful red-headed fairy with green wings. She looks at Bob and tells him that he is the most beautiful unicorn she has ever seen. Then you see a watercolor illustration of Bob, and he is indeed a majestic unicorn with sparkles surrounding him.

At this point, the reader questions why all his friends never understood that Bob was indeed a unicorn. Until you turn the page.

You see that the whole time Bob was just a baby elephant with a paper towel roll tied atop his head as a pretend horn. The fairy was a little girl pretending to be a beautiful fairy.

You see, they saw each other and instantly "got" each other. They were the same type of beings, and they used their imaginations the same way. They were living from the heart, and people doing that recognize each other. It is an energy we can feel in each other.

Bob Is a Unicorn is a book about real life.

One day, you might be listening to the whispers in your heart. Doing the things that bring you joy, being *you*. And guess what? Not everybody is going to get you. Not everybody is going to support you. Some people will make it their mission to try to break your spirit and ignore your heart.

It is hard not to listen to the people who tell us how our dreams might fail. People who tell us how there's so little chance of success that we may as well not even try. What if I had listened to all the people who told me how hard it is to make a career out of creating picture books for children? What if I had paid attention to the statistic that only 2 percent of author/illustrators can make a living from their book sales? I would not be writing this book.

Life is not about statistics. Life is not about playing it safe. Life is about trying things to find out what brings us joy and passion. It is about playing and having fun. And yes, it is also about failing and messing up. Honestly, if we don't want any of the hard times, what is the point? We aren't going to learn and grow when nothing challenges us.

I want to remind you that I am in one of those challenging times right now. If I had written this book a year ago, it would have been a very different book. My definition of success in life was so tied to my financial success that I saw no difference. I had to lose my income quickly and drastically to learn an essential lesson. I am the same person with or without money. I love to inspire children. I love to create stories and art for children to make them feel safe, included, and loved.

I needed my money to go away so I could understand that my magic exists with or without it. I needed to remember that my heart will always lead me down the right path when I trust it. It wasn't until I truly learned this lesson and felt it deep in my soul that I knew I could write this book.

And heck, I don't even know if this book is going to sell or not. But for the first time, I don't care. I am writing this because I need to hear these words. I need to share these words with others. If even one single person out there understands that they deserve to have a magical, joyful life just because they exist, then it was worth writing this book.

You deserve to be you. You deserve to live this life exactly as you were made. You deserve to create and enjoy your magical life the way you want to live it. No one else gets to decide who you are but you.

When you begin to believe this and really listen to your heart, two pretty amazing things happen. First? Your people find you. There is a huge world of people out there, and your people are waiting to find you and support you. Your people may think like you, act like you, use their imaginations just like you.

Or they might not get you at all but totally respect you and love you exactly as you are. For instance, my husband does not understand my brain and that I hang out with and have imaginary conversations with the characters in my head. I don't understand how he can study calculus for 'fun' or look at lines and lines of computer code and finds it fascinating. We choose to respect and love each other while not understanding each other all the time. Thank goodness.

Hang in there and trust who you are. Trust the things that give you joy. If ever you are sitting alone in your room thinking, *No one gets me. I'm too weird. I'm too different.* I promise you are not. This world is huge. If you are reading this book and resonating with it, then you have your people already. Go to MNScreative.com, join my social media, find me. I am your people. My people are your people. I promise.

The second thing that happens when you stay true to yourself and listen to your heart?

That, my friends, is when you'll begin to notice and recognize the magic. Life just seems to somehow get easier. You naturally begin to stop worrying about the how of it all and just know that life is happening *for* you, not *to* you.

Trust in who you are in this world. You'll see.

"When I was a boy and I would see scary things in the news, my mother would say to me, 'Look for the helpers. You will always find people who are helping.'"

-Fred Rogers

19

Look for Your Mouse People

WANT TO KNOW A secret? I am not a people person. Okay, that is a lie. I love to be around people but only when it is my choice. But isn't that all of us really? That's why I love the life of a writer. I work alone, but I am never lonely. I love to hang out with my characters and daydream with them all day.

However, that also makes it really hard for me to ask for help. When you have had to make your own way from a very young age, you tend to become very independent. Throw in a job where you work alone, and it can be very difficult when you need to ask for help.

When I hired my editor for my picture books, I was asking for help. I had to admit I could not figure it out on my own. It was humbling, but it made all the difference. I have the career I do now because of asking for help.

Hiring an editor may not seem like asking for help, but you feel vulnerable when you hand over your baby. I hate waiting for feedback on my writing. I loathe it. Just thinking about handing this manuscript over to my editor in a few days gives me anxiety. Ew. I hate this feeling. I'm going to stop thinking about it now.

Being vulnerable does not feel good. Hearing other's opinions can be hard. I have learned that the feedback that makes me angry is usually the feedback that I need to pay attention to the most. I get angry when I hear the truth. I have learned to recognize anger from feedback as my heart telling me to pause and listen. Whether it is from a friend, my spouse, or an editor, I have learned a truth I need to hear initially makes me angry.

Speaking of spouses making you angry... I have a wonderful husband. I love Kevin very much. We also make each other angry a lot. He is possibly the most opposite person to me on the planet. That can make for a very difficult marriage after a while. We see the world very differently. He is a careful, left-brained realist, and I am a chaotic, right-brained optimist.

Last year, after three stressful moves in six years and many life events, we really began to have problems. For the first time I wondered if we might not make it. I suggested therapy, and my husband was all for it. Let me tell you, asking for help was the best thing we ever could have done. I cannot recommend therapy enough.

Remember when I said I'd get back to household finances and how my husband and I deal with money? Here we are. Some might think it odd that my husband and I have kept our finances very separate. I want to explain how it happened.

This is the second marriage for both of us. When my first marriage ended, I decided, quite consciously, and probably quite unhealthily, that I would never again rely on a partner. I would never again put myself in a position to be with someone who would let me down financially. My husband on the other hand, had been taken great advantage of by his former wife. She didn't work and had spent money freely and with no concern for the debt it put them in.

When we met, we were perfect for each other. I was a highly independent woman who made it clear I did not want or need his money and he was leery of a woman who wanted to date him because he made a good living. We were a perfect financial storm.

We kept our finances separate. I paid for everything for the kids. Their clothes, their activities, their presents. I proudly paid for their cars and their college expenses. (How I overcompensated because of the guilt of making them children of divorce is a much longer story and could be a whole other book.)

What we created in our partnership was a financial separateness that eventually caused quite an emotional separateness. We had never dealt with financial stress in our marriage until my business slowed down because we always had enough money. Once we had some financial issues though, all our past issues and the years of emotional separation took their toll.

We had both never worked through the damage our past marriages had done to us. We had never owned up to the damage we contributed to in our past marriages either.

We could not have any discussion about money without it devolving into a terrible fight. We could not communicate without bringing up hurts in the past from our exes and each other.

I am so grateful we decided to try therapy.

But beware. When we started therapy, I was sure that our therapist was going to roll her eyes and tell my husband how ridiculous he was being and how much he had to change to save our marriage.

Um. That isn't exactly what happened.

Hi. It's me. I'm the problem, it's me. (Thank you, Taylor Swift, for my personal anthem.)

Okay, it's not *all* me. It's quite literally both of us. But when I realized the things *I* needed to be accountable for and how *my* actions and *my* reactions were affecting my husband, it really changed things for us. Do you know about love languages? If not, look them up. It will really help you out!

Geez Louise, maybe find out before you get married if you have completely different love languages. I want to be hugged and touched and told I am beautiful and talented all day long.

Words of affirmation and touch are my love languages. My husband's main love language is acts of service. So if I put all the new patio furniture together and clean the garage out without asking him for his help, he is one happy husband!

Now we understand each other so much better. We each try to communicate and do things in the way the other understands and appreciates. We are still in therapy and I'm not sure we will, or should ever stop. It helps us so much. Don't be afraid to ask for help.

Also, people like to help. Some people love to help. Sometimes they just need to know you need the help. I am so grateful for the helpers in this world like Mouse from my picture book *Dog and Mouse.*

In *Dog and Mouse,* there's this little yellow dog who keeps coming to the same spot in the woods each day. She sits there all day long, just watching and waiting for something.

A tiny gray mouse notices this dog every day. She finally gets so curious that she just must know what's going on. Mouse finally goes up to Dog and asks what she is doing.

Dog looks at Mouse and says that she's busy looking for her best friend. Mouse gets very excited and offers to help, declaring that "helping is her favorite and very best skill!" Dog is touched by the offer and says Mouse is welcome to stay and help search.

Day after day, the little mouse shows up to help the dog look. Days become months, and you see them playing together, celebrating holidays, and sharing treats as Mouse wonders what Dog's best friend might look like.

Eventually, an entire year goes by, and it's the anniversary of the day Mouse began to help Dog. Dog goes to their meeting spot, but Mouse is nowhere to be found. This is unusual; Mouse has never been late or missed a day. Dog begins musing about their time together and starts to get worried. Dog decides to search for Mouse.

Just then, Dog sees Mouse coming down the path. Mouse was just a bit late; she was picking up treats.

That's the moment Dog realizes that Mouse is the friend she has been looking for this whole time.

I adore that little Mouse so much because she didn't help Dog to get anything out of it. She helped Dog just because she *could*. Mouse was honestly shocked that she turned out to be Dog's best friend—the one not even Dog had realized she was searching for.

Remember, sometimes the helpers you need are right there in front of you, waiting to be noticed. Thank goodness for the Mouse People in this world. They are the helpers, and this world couldn't survive without them.

Look for Your Mouse People

"She knew just who she was,
knew who she could be,
and this belief in herself,
set Cordelia free."

-Michelle Nelson-Schmidt

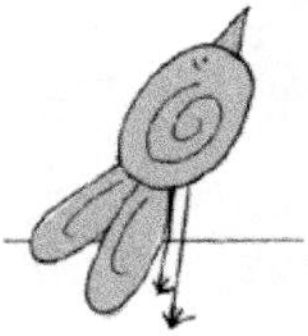

20

Fly Like Cordelia

WHEN YOU DISCOVER YOUR purpose and joy, figure out what makes your heart shine and own who you get to be in this world, you want to share that with the world. When you let your light shine, you make the whole world brighter and more magical too.

Here is what happens when you begin to figure out who you are in this world. You've done the hard part. You've tried things, you've failed, you've gotten back up again. You've made mistakes and you've learned. You've paid your dues and you've practiced. You've asked for help and you've overcome. Now is your time to shine, baby!

You know who you are in this world, and you own it. You are lighting the path for others, and you want to share your secret with the world. "Listen to your heart!" you want to scream. "Find your joy!"

Honestly, things are so good when you start listening to your heart, trusting it, and doing the things that bring you joy. It's so magical that it almost feels like you can fly. How can you not share the secret with others? It seems selfish not to share this secret to joyful living, right?

But watch out. Where there is joy, there are Joy Squashers. Beware the Joy Squashers, my friends!

That's exactly why I wrote my picture book *Cordelia*.

Cordelia is a little red-haired girl who can fly. She flies and sings with the birds. She races pelicans over the ocean and flies up to the moon to play games with the stars. Flying is what gives Cordelia joy. It is what makes Cordelia feel most herself. She feels magical just because she gets to be her. Cordelia loves who she is and who she gets to be in this world.

You are also supposed to love who *you* are and who *you* get to be in this world. We all are supposed to love who we are and who we get to be in this world.

It is not about how much money we make. It is not about how powerful we are. It is not about how many followers we have or how many people like us.

Life is about you loving *yourself.*

Life is about knowing you are *enough*.

Life is about knowing that you *matter* just because you exist.

You exist, and that alone is a magical, joyful thing.

When you do the things that bring you joy—singing out loud, playing an instrument, drawing a picture, walking in the woods, planting a garden, cooking a meal, reading a book—you are doing exactly what you are supposed to be doing. If we are not loving, playing, and being joyful, what is the point of human existence?

Life is always going to hand us hard times. Sad and tragic things are always going to happen. However, it is up to us to create the love and the joy and the magic to help us through the inevitable dark and sad times.

I can promise you that there is joy and light to be found even in the darkest times. You might not be ready to see it, but it is waiting for you to discover it when you are ready. The joy makes the dark times bearable.

I have to tell you something again. I told you earlier, but I need to remind you of it. Even though I have no formal training or degree, I know I am right. Are you ready?

You are enough. Exactly as you are. You are allowed to feel joy without it making you money. You are allowed to feel joy just because it feels good. We are supposed to feel joy, and we don't have to earn it. *We do not have to earn joy.*

But.

There's always a but, right? We can feel joy only if we allow it.

When Cordelia found her joy, she tried to share it. She tried to tell everyone and anyone who would listen that they could fly too. They could be joyful just because they wanted to be joyful.

That's when the Joy Squashers showed up. They told her that people don't fly. They told her it was impossible. They told her she was silly.

And Cordelia believed them.

Other people made Cordelia doubt herself. Once she believed that, she could no longer fly. Her world became gray. She missed her friends. She missed herself.

Until one day, she thought about how much she missed her old life. A righteous anger filled her. Cordelia was mad at herself. After all, no one made her stop believing in herself. When she listened to others, she gave away her power. Which meant she could take it back.

Spoiler alert! Cordelia took her power back. She began to sing and play and soar again.

Once again, real life rears its ugly head in my picture books. Whether it's other people who are not ready to feel their own joy and magic, or it's your own doubtful voice in your head, there will unfortunately always be Joy Squashers. These people want to extinguish your light, dim your joy, and dull your sparkle.

You can't let them. When the Joy Squashers come, you need to remember who you are. You need to remember this book. You need to remember me and how much I believe in you and your magic in this world. I am writing this book to remember my magic again too.

This world is a hard place to live in. Remembering who you are and holding on to your joy and magic are things we are all going to have to do over and over and over again. It is the price we need to be willing to pay to be here. The lesson of joy is going to be a lifelong quest but one that gets easier and easier.

The world needs you so very much. The way I see it, we are all puzzle pieces in the same giant puzzle. Have you ever gotten to the end of a one thousand piece puzzle and you can't find the last piece? It's awful, right? All that work to get it all together and then not getting the satisfaction of putting in the very last piece? That tiny missing piece creates a gaping hole in the big picture.

Without me, without you, the picture cannot be finished. We are all needed and all equally important.

Don't you ever doubt for one single second how important you are or how much you matter in this world. Find your joy and go fly, knowing how much you matter. No one can take that away from you without your permission.

"Well, your greatest joy definitely comes from doing something for another, especially when it was done with no thought of something in return."

-John Wooden

21

Spread Love Like Herman

DURING SCHOOL VISITS, CHILDREN ask me all kinds of questions: how old I am, how many kids I have, or if I have any pets.

Occasionally a child, usually a very young one, asks me a poignant question. Once a five-year-old asked me what I would do if I could not make books for kids anymore. I had to stop and think. I had to really think about it.

What would I do if I could not do what I loved for a living? What if I lost the ability to draw? What if an accident took my right hand? I could still tell stories. I could dictate them onto the computer. But what if I couldn't speak? What if I lost my career? Who am I without my job?

That answer is the reason I am writing this book. Only now do I realize I already figured out the answer when I wrote my picture book *Herman: A Little Story about Spreading Love.*

Originally I wrote this story in 2015. I was on a school visit up north, and an old college friend came by my hotel to visit. She brought a "hotel picnic" with her. She had fruit, cheese, crackers, jellies, and bread. We put out the food, and I picked up spreadable cheese for crackers. My friend said, "Oh no! I forgot to bring a knife!"

I exclaimed, "Wait!" I rummaged through my purse and held up a metal butter knife.

"Um, why do you have a butter knife in your purse?" she asked.

The truth was, I had no idea. But I quickly said, "A butter knife is a really versatile tool! It can spread cheese, sure, but it can also be a screwdriver, a hammer, or a lever. It can even clean a hairbrush. Everyone should carry one!"

I went and washed it, and we happily ate our little picnic.

When I got home, I drew a picture of a cute butter knife. I named him Herman after a very nice Boston cop who helped me navigate the city train system while I was up there. (I doubt he will ever read this book, but if you know a cop up in the city of Boston named Herman, tell him he has inspired many to spread love!) I posted the little drawing on Facebook with the caption, "All Herman ever wanted to do was spread the love."

My friends on Facebook fell in love with Herman. I decided to challenge myself to write a story about him in time for Storytime Live, a Facebook Live show I started that year and still do every Wednesday evening. I told everyone on Facebook that I would have a whole story about Herman that night.

All day long I tried to come up with a story idea about Herman. The hours ticked by, but no ideas came. As showtime drew near, I realized I was not going to come up with a story in time. I decided I would just tell the kids that sometimes you set a goal and you don't achieve it. It would be a great lesson to let kids know that the world doesn't end when you don't achieve a goal.

Once I gave myself permission to not hit my goal, a storyline popped into my head. Isn't that always the way? We relax and forget about a problem, and that is when inspiration hits. Why don't we relax more and just trust the process, right? With just an hour before Storytime, I wrote out Herman's story.

In the story, Herman lives in a kitchen, and the owner of the kitchen uses him a lot. She spreads butter on toast in the morning, peanut butter and jelly on bread in the afternoons, and honey on apples as a snack. On the best days, she uses Herman to spread warm gooey cheese on hot squishy bread. When Herman gets used, he notices that he makes people happy. Herman equates how happy he makes people feel with his importance. He thinks of himself as spreading love when he spreads food.

While many other utensils and kitchen appliances also get used, Herman decides that he has, by far, the most important purpose in the kitchen. Spreading love is an important purpose, after all.

But one day something happens. The owner of the house decides she needs to eat healthier. She gets a blender and starts drinking fruit and vegetable smoothies. Stanley the blender is the new star of the kitchen. Herman hardly ever gets taken out of the drawer anymore, while everyone marvels at the shiny new blender.

Herman goes to a very dark place, both literally and figuratively. He closes himself up in the kitchen drawer and laments the loss of his purpose in life. Just as he decides there's no reason to go on, he hears a yell for help. It's coming from the piano keys in the living room!

He jumps out of the drawer and sees three piano keys all stuck down. Herman hurries over, slides himself between two keys, leans a bit for leverage, and gets the keys unstuck.

Then he hears a screw complaining from the other room about how loose he is. Herman hurries over there and screws him back into the wall. He looks around for others needing some help.

He helps a penny get out of a floorboard, he helps a mason jar get her lid unstuck with a few light taps, he gets hair out of a hairbrush, and he scrapes some gum off the carpet.

After helping out all of his friends, Herman realizes that he has so many more purposes than just spreading food. Most importantly, he realizes that helping his friends feels just like spreading love. (Clearly, Herman's main love language is acts of service!)

Herman discovered that spreading love and joy is the most important purpose of all. Anyone might lose one of our purposes in life, like a job or a certain ability. But we can never, ever lose our main purpose in life—to love and help others.

In 2015 when I wrote Herman, I had figured out what true success was, but somehow through the years, I lost my way. I am so grateful I found my way back to this knowledge.

Joy and love. To be joyful, to be loved, and to love others are the most important things we can do as humans. If we do those three things, we have achieved ultimate success as human beings. This is, and will always be from now on, *my* definition of a successful life.

When I stray from this definition of success, it's easy to tell. I'm living in my head, I'm worrying about things out of my control, I'm not loving myself, I'm not doing things that bring me joy, or I'm not looking to see how I can serve, help, and love others. As soon as I begin doing any and all of those things? My life gets back on track immediately, as if by–you know I'm going to say it–*magic*.

"Joy is not in things; it is in us."

-Richard Wagner

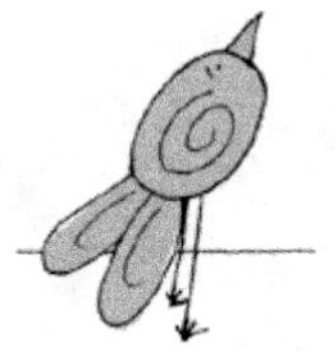

22

Love Yourself Most of All

As I get to the last chapter of this book, it occurs to me that maybe I didn't need to write this book at all. I've already written down all the lessons I needed to learn in my picture books.

So many children and adults have written to me through the years, telling me how much my books and their messages have meant to them. I thought I was writing them for children, but I think I've written these books to the child I was and the books she needed to read. My picture books are love notes to my past selves and are reminders for my future selves.

When I look back, I realize my books tell the story of my life, from the poor young mom who found her strength in motherhood and painting pet portraits to the accomplished author and illustrator of thirty-two published books today. The books tell my stories and my lessons learned. I guess some lessons you just need to learn repeatedly.

The best thing that ever happened to me was almost going out of business and losing my income streams. It woke me up and taught me some of the most important lessons of my life so far; Joy does not need to be earned and being a successful human being has nothing to do with money.

This past year has been one of the hardest of my life, both because of what I've shared with you in this book, and because of events I cannot share because they are not my stories to tell. I have no idea how everything is going to turn out. That once excited me. Then it began to scare me. Now I am excited by all the possibilities and wonderful 'what ifs' once again. What amazing moments lie ahead? What magic will I create? What new joys will I discover? What new messes will I make? What new mistakes will I endure? What new failures will I experience? I welcome them *all*.

I hope you are asking yourself these same questions. When we leave behind fear and embrace the unknown with playfulness and joy, we can be sure to know that magic awaits all of us.

At the end of each school visit, I ask if the children will help me continue to create more magic in the world by making my Pinkie Promise. I have over a million of these from children and adults across the country. Now that you have heard my story, it feels right to ask you to make my Pinkie Promise, too.

Just raise up your pinkie and say it along with me: *"I promise I will follow my heart and follow my dreams with everything I've got. No matter what—no matter what if!"*

If ever you begin to forget yourself, I hope you reread this book or any of my picture books to help you remember the beautiful, magical, successful human being that you are.

Use your Whatif Monster when you're scared, believe in yourself as much as Bob, and look for your Mouse People when you need help. But most of all, remember to love yourself on your hard and messy days. Love yourself most of all on the days you've made such a big mistake, you're not even sure how you're going to fix it.

When you love yourself like that? You get those incredible, fantastical days that I think probably feel just as magical as flying like Cordelia.

Finally, when you struggle with what your purpose in this life might be, remember my sweet friend Herman. The ultimate purpose we all have on this earth with this gift of life we have been given, is to spread love to ourselves and others. No one can ever take that purpose away from any of us.

Thank you

Thank you so much for taking the time to read my book. If you enjoyed it, I humbly request you to review it on my website at MNScreative.com, on Amazon, or Goodreads. Or all three!

Reviews have a huge impact on whether other readers choose to read a book as well or even get seen on sites like Amazon. I thank you sincerely in advance for taking a few extra minutes to leave me honest reviews.

Also, I ask you to please share my book with your book groups (see discussion questions on the next page), classes, friends, and anyone else you think might enjoy or benefit from reading it.

I also welcome feedback directly from my readers! I would love to hear from you! You can email me at michelle@mnscreative.com

Acknowledgements

I cannot adequately put in writing how grateful and thankful I am to my beloved Beta Readers and Launch Team. This was a very personal and vulnerable book to write and they created such a safe space for me to share it. They took time out of their busy lives to read this book the moment it was ready. They gave thoughtful, detailed feedback that made this book so much better than it ever would have been without their input. I'm truly grateful for the grammar zealots in the group who caught every typo, extra space, and missing space. If you found any in this book, it is the fault of the author and any last changes I made without asking them to review the final, final, FINAL draft.

I want to thank my editor Catherine Findlay who said yes to a very quick turn-around to do line edits of this book so I could get it quickly to my Beta Readers in order to hit my publishing deadline. Catherine also edited my Whatif Monster Chapter Book Series and I could not recommend her more. She's an incredibly talented editor and her insights on story arc and character are invaluable. You can find her on Reedsy.com if you're looking for an excellent editor for children's fiction.

I want to thank my husband, Kevin, who doesn't always agree with me, doesn't always understand me, is not a super fan of my over-sharing nature, but has never wavered in supporting me. He allows me to be who I am in this world even when it makes our marriage (and finances) more difficult. He's my best friend in the world and I love him endlessly. I'm so grateful I get to share this adventure we call life together.

Finally, I want to thank the hard times in my life. I hate them when I'm going through them, but once I'm on the other side, I am always so much better off. The most difficult, dark and hopeless times have given me the gift of understanding true joy and my worth as a human being in this world. I hope my story helps you see your joy and worth during the storms that life gives you. I hope maybe my words help get you to the other side a little bit easier knowing you are not alone.

Discussion Questions for Book Clubs/Classes

1. What was your favorite part of the book?
2. What was your least favorite?
3. Did you race to the end, or did you read it slowly and take your time?
4. Which part has stuck with you the most?
5. What did you think of the writing? Are there any standout sentences?
6. Did you reread any passages? If so, which ones?
7. Would you want to read another book by this author?
8. Did reading the book impact your mood? If yes, how so?
9. What surprised you most about the book?
10. How did your opinion of the book change as you read it?
11. If you could ask the author anything, what would it be?
12. How does the book's title work in relation to the book's contents? If you could give the book a new title, what would it be?

13. Did this book remind you of any other books?
14. How did it impact you? Do you think you'll remember it in a few months or years?
15. Would you ever consider re-reading it? Why or why not?
16. Who do you most want to read this book?
17. Are there lingering questions from the book you can't stop thinking about?
18. Did the book strike you as original?

Other Titles by Michelle Nelson-Schmidt

Dogs, Dogs!

Cats, Cats!

Jonathan James and the Whatif Monster

Bob is a Unicorn

Dog and Mouse

Cordelia

Cordelia and the Whale

What If I Know My Shapes

What If I Know My Opposites

What If I Know My Feelings

What If I Know How to Be Kind

The Whatif Monster Early Reader Chapter Book Series (18 books)

Please, Mind the Bear

Herman: A Little Story About Spreading Love

M is for Monsters: What If I Know My Alphabet

Where to Purchase MNS Books

Purchase Directly from Michelle

Scan the QR Code below with your phone to be brought to MNScreative.com

Buy From Amazon

Scan the QR Code below with your phone to be brought to Michelle's Amazon Author Central Page

Independent Book Stores

Independently owned bookstores and shops. can contact Michelle directly for wholesale pricing or through her book distributer, Ingram Content Group.

Just a Lil' Something Extra

CPSIA information can be obtained
at www.ICGtesting.com
Printed in the USA
JSHW060928070623
42856JS00004B/7

9 781952 013713